SURVIVAL NOTES
FOR GRADUATES

INSPIRATION FOR THE
ULTIMATE JOURNEY

SURVIVAL NOTES FOR GRADUATES

INSPIRATION FOR THE ULTIMATE JOURNEY

BY
ROBERT STOFEL

Ambassador Books, Inc.
Worcester • Massachusetts

Library of Congress Cataloging-in-Publication Data

Stofel, Robert, 1962-
  Survival notes for graduates : inspiration for the ultimate journey / by Robert Stofel.
    p. cm.
  ISBN 1-929039-22-0 (pbk.)
  1. Youth--Religious life. 2. Youth--Conduct of life. I. Title.

  BV4531.3.S76 2004
  248.8'34--dc22

                        200400178

Published in the United States by Ambassador Books, Inc.,
91 Prescott Street, Worcester, Massachusetts 01605 • (800) 577-0909

Printed in the United States of America.
For current information about all titles from Ambassador Books, Inc.,
visit our website at: www.ambassadorbooks.com.

Dedicated with love and affection
to my daughters, Blair and Sloan,
who inspired the creation of this book.

CONTENTS

Acknowledgements

This book first existed as individual devotionals that were written to my daughters. My oldest daughter, Blair, and I exchanged a journal her first year in college at the University of Alabama. I would write a devotional in the journal, and then I would mail it off to her. She would make an entry and return it. Then I would write another and repeat the process.

Soon after Blair's first year of college, I began writing to my youngest daughter, Sloan. Then two years later, I sent a book proposal with sample chapters to Jennifer Conlan at Ambassador Books. She contacted me and offered helpful suggestions. After much revising and endless support from the team at Ambassador Books, you hold the result. I thank them for their dedication and determination. They enhanced the book with their hearts and souls.

I thank my wife, Jill, who knows all about me and loves me anyway. She kept me encouraged along the way.

Thanks to my quasi-marketing team—Kaye Waller, Kathy Winton, and Kathy Delancey. You accepted the challenge to carry the message of this book like a circuit rider. And I'm deeply moved by your dedication.

Thanks to Mom and Nick for their love and encouragement.

Thanks to Hickory Hills Community Church. You're the wind beneath my wings. Without you I would be nothing special. With you I'm complete.

Thanks to Nathan O'Neal for suggesting I write this book. And thanks for an unbelievable website: www.robertstofel.com. I love it!

Thanks to my spiritual advisors, Roy Clarke, Jim Waller, and Bruce Coble. Your encouragement and guidance are priceless.

Thanks to my friends in Franklin, Tennessee, and Decatur, Alabama. You know who you are. I love you dearly.

INTRODUCTION

Congratulations! You are stepping forward into a brave new world. And the road begins with questions and uncertainty. Will I fit in at college? Am I ready to leave home? What is on the other side of graduation? Will I survive? These questions are normal. You are sprouting wings—wings that will establish how high you can soar and how low you can fly. It will be a time of exhilaration and learning. You are embarking on a year in your life that will be like no other. And you will survive it. Each devotional in this book will help guide you through. God's light for your path will be revealed. So relax. Travel this new road with assurance.

> May you be infused with strength and purity,
> filled with confidence . . .
> — *1 Thessalonians 3:13, MSG*

How can we understand the road we travel?
It is the Lord who directs our steps.

— *Proverbs 20:24, NLT*

ONE

THE EDGE OF GRADUATION

*G*raduation is a rite-of-passage—the last hurdle of adolescence. And the question that will form in your mind as the toss of caps and hugs from classmates fade into a new beginning will be: "How can I understand the road I'll travel?" Every life is littered with uncertainty, doubt, and lonely valleys, but don't let feelings of insecurity stop you from dreaming. Proceed with your hopes and dreams, and if you get confused, God will direct your path.

The temptation of the future is to let circumstances guide us. But circumstances are the puff of dreamy clouds. They move with the wind and cannot be trusted. The three guiding elements to look for in a successful life are faith, hope, and love. These are the values that simply and romantically hold the fibers of our dreams together. A life built around these three will never lose its way.

The future belongs to those who
believe in the beauty of their dreams.
— *Eleanor Roosevelt*

They sow the wind,
and reap the whirlwind.

—※—

— *Hosea 8:7, NIV*

TWO

HOW TO BE FREE OF YOUR PARENTS

$\mathcal{B}$y now you understand freedom is a mirage, a mere swapping of the guards. You are free, but not free. You are free of Mom's constant badgering, but that freedom comes with a new price. There will be no more home cooking. And don't think Dad will foot the bill you rack up at the bar. Life at college will take on new responsibilities. Expect this. You have to understand freedom has its price. So be careful. Don't throw responsibility to the wind. You may reap a whirlwind.

Stop going to places that don't fulfill just because you have the freedom to do so. Be honest with yourself. Step back and ask for discernment. Then take on this new responsibility. It is a lot easier to submit now than fail later. You know what will happen if the grades are low. You will reap the whirlwind. Then it will be nobody's responsibility but your own.

> Freedom is a mirage on the desert. If you reach the place
> it seemed to be, you will find it dry, because being free means
> that you are no longer needed or loved by others.
> — *Josephine Lowman*

You keep track of all my sorrows.
You have collected all my tears
in your bottle.

— *Psalm 56:8, NLT*

THREE
WHAT TO CRY OVER

$\mathcal{T}$here will be good days and bad days. Graduation is not a deliverance from sorrow. Cloudy days happen. Jobs can be lost and relationships will be broken. Sorrow happens.

A passage in one of Tennyson's poems says:

> So runs my dreams; but what am I?
> An infant crying in the night;
> An infant crying for the light;
> And with no language but a cry.

Tennyson says, ". . . but what am I?" It will be during days of sorrow that you will ask yourself this question. Never doubt yourself on these days. Tell yourself that this too shall pass. There will be new people to date and jobs to be had. The sea is full and everybody is looking. So don't get down on yourself. Don't lose your smile. The day will always begin again and so will your life.

> You have to live through your pain gradually
> and thus deprive it of its power over you.
> — *Henri Nouwen*

If you plot evil, you will be lost; but if you plan good, you will be granted unfailing love and faithfulness.

— *Proverbs 14:22, NLT*

FOUR

WHEN WILL YOU MEET YOUR REAL LOVE?

*A*vailability for the moment is not planning for good. There is no need to get desperate. You've just graduated. Take some time. The right love will come into your life at the right moment. Your life has been written before the foundations of the world.

The way to "plan good" is to save your love. Be faithful today for tomorrow. This is the difficult part. It will take focus. You will have days of doubt. But don't stop planning or dreaming of love. Take action and pray for your future mate on a daily basis. This is the first step in a wonderful plan of waiting on the right love. So stay calm and stick to your plan.

> Love at first sight deserves a second look.
> — *Unknown*

You're hopeless, you religion scholars and Pharisees! Frauds! You're like manicured grave plots, grass clipped and the flowers bright, but six feet down it's all rotting bones and worm-eaten flesh.

— Matthew 23:27, MSG

FIVE
FAKE IDS

Fakes are in the world. They wear Harley-Davidson T-shirts and act like tough guys. But they don't even own a Harley. People can be so fake. So can Rolex watches and Oakley sunglasses. Fakes are everywhere you want to go. They are even in church. They were around in Jesus' day. And Jesus scorned fakes. He called them "Frauds!" He said they were rotting bones and worm-eaten flesh. Jesus did not pull any punches. He called them the way He saw them.

Turn on certain religious television programs. Fake as can be. So please don't add to the number. There is nothing to be gained. Be true. Be honest with God. Don't go around flashing a fake ID. There are people watching, and they know a fake when they see one. This is why they don't go to church. They don't want to sit with a bunch of hypocrites. Let's do something about it. Let's be real.

Preach the Gospel at all times and when necessary use words.
— *St. Francis of Assisi*

$\mathcal{A}$nd the ugly and gaunt cows ate up
the seven fine looking and fat cows.
So Pharaoh awoke.

— *Genesis 41:4*

SIX

HOW TO BE FAT AS A COW AND HAPPY

Pharaoh's Stephen-King-novel-like-nightmare would have probably been interpreted by Freud as some type of paranoia. Vicious cows gobbled up the genuine ones. The skinny fed upon the fat, and if you're a cow, fat is good. Cows are the only ones praised for robust rumps. They never hear, "Lose some weight, why don't you." In the pasture, fat is good, and in your soul, fat is even better.

A good way to beat back the gaunt cows is to live God's way. "But what happens when we live God's way? He brings gifts into our lives, much the same way that fruit appears in an orchard— things like affection for others, exuberance about life, serenity. We develop a willingness to stick with things . . . involved in loyal commitments, not needing to force our way in life, able to marshal and direct our energies wisely" (Galatians 5:22-23, MSG).

Living God's way will kill the ugly and gaunt cows.

> The great essentials of happiness are something to do,
> something to love, and something to hope for.
> — *Alexander Chalmers*

$\mathcal{D}$on't let your great riches mislead you . . .

—*Job 36:18*, MSG

SEVEN

Beware of Materialism's Lure

$\mathcal{M}$aterialism will entice you when you graduate and move away from home. There will be a season of amassing stuff to stock your dorm or apartment. And it will be liberating, a wonderful joy! So enjoy it. But beware of materialism's lure. It is the opium of our times. Don't fall for the lie that happiness is wrapped in a killer job and a house in the suburbs—complete with a swimming pool, surround-sound, and a BMW in the garage. These things are nice. But it is a lure to a greater vastness—an open grave that never says, "Enough."

Money is not evil. It is the love of money that is evil. And when we love money more than people, we build bigger houses. We forget that people in Third World countries are starving. This is the decadence of wasting money on self. But there is nothing wrong with asking God to meet your needs. He wants us to pray, "Give us today our daily bread" (Matthew 6:11, NIV). He loves to answer this prayer.

Two watermelons cannot be held under one arm.
— *Turkish Proverb*

My guilt overwhelms me—it is
a burden too heavy to bear.

— *Psalm 38:4, NLT*

EIGHT

CARRYING THE LUGGAGE OF GUILT

*T*here are things we carry—luggage, babies, firewood, ChapStick in our pockets, fake Kate Spade bags—real ones, too. Then there are things we pull—boats, trailers, horses, racecars, and people to places they would just as soon not go. We are a people of the carry, haul and pull.

Then there is guilt, a burden too heavy to bear. Carrying guilt will deplete us. Thinking guilty thoughts will not change things. Accept where you are and ask forgiveness. Put it behind you. Do what Paul did, ". . . I am focusing all my energies on this one thing: Forgetting the past and looking forward to what lies ahead . . ." (Philippians 3:13, NLT). Set yourself free. Don't waste another moment beating yourself up. Put guilt down. Walk away.

> The guilty catch themselves.
> — *Ancient Proverb*

*Listening to gossip is like eating
cheap candy; do you really want junk
like that in your belly?*

— *Proverbs 18:8, MSG*

NINE
HAVE YOU HEARD?

*H*ave you heard? Gossip is a boomerang. It will come back to haunt you. But this never seems to stop us. We are a people of a loose tongue, living in a gossip society. Television shows thrive on it. Tabloids divulge it. We love to gossip. We love to talk about other people's problems. It makes us feel better about ourselves. Our problems don't seem so big. "We're not that bad," we say.

Gossip seems harmless. But when it leads to damaged relationships, it is a killer. It murders friendships and casts doubt on whether or not you can be trusted. So always remember this simple rule. If someone gossips about others to your face, they will talk about you behind your back. This is their MO. So don't say something you will regret later. For gossip is a boomerang. It will come back to bite you.

> Who gossips to you will gossip of you.
> — *Turkish Proverb*

*L*ate one afternoon David got out of bed after taking a nap and went for a stroll on the roof of the palace. As he looked out over the city, he noticed a woman of unusual beauty taking a bath.

— *2 Samuel 11:1-2, NLT*

TEN

KEEPING YOUR CLOTHES ON

*A*fternoon naps were the most significant item on David's royal schedule. He had conquered most of his foes. He had been translated from the shepherd's darkness into a royal light. And he allowed his life to lull into sweet afternoons of lovemaking with another man's wife.

You can expect a lull after graduation. So be careful. Don't fall into the same trap as David. Keep striving for victory over the daily battles of lust—sexually and materialistically—because bathing in the waters of every life is a bitter snare that touts: "Go ahead, lust. You're a graduate! Look around at all the people who are finding love. Who needs marriage? Have an afternoon of lovemaking. No one will care."

Nothing was ever the same for David. God sent this message: "From this time on, the sword will be a constant threat to your family" (2 Samuel 12:10, NLT). His afternoon lovemaking opened the door for tragedy. And it rolled through his family, killing, robbing and destroying.

Give me chastity and continence, but do not give it yet.
— *St. Augustine, in* CONFESSIONS

---

*Then I saw the Lamb standing
on Mount Zion . . .*

—※—

— Revelation 14:1, NLT

ELEVEN
GREAT BEAUTY TIPS

 ℐhere are breathtaking sights—sunrises, sunsets, waves crashing into a heap of foam on rocky seashores. Then there is magnificent beauty that has nothing to do with external flash. The Apostle John first looked, then he beheld. Learning what to look for in a person is an act of beholding, not seeing. Sights are seen. Beauty is beheld. Wealth is a beauty with a shell but no kernel. Look for inner magnificence, which will contain the Spirit of God. Beauty that takes our breath away is when we discover the Lamb of God standing on the Mount Zion of our lover's soul.

> Beauty, unaccompanied by virtue,
> is as a flower without perfume.
> — *From the French*

So Elijah went and found Elisha son of Shaphat plowing a field with a team of oxen. There were eleven teams of oxen ahead of him, and he was plowing with the twelfth team. Elijah went over to him and threw his cloak across his shoulders . . .

— *1 Kings 19:19, NLT*

TWELVE

THE STENCH OF YOUR PRESENT CRISIS

Elisha was a plowboy with dirt beneath his fingernails and calluses on his hands and sweat beads lodged in his sideburns. He lived with his parents and farmed the fertile soil on the back forty acres. He was doing the honorable thing. He was respecting his family's needs. And he probably hated it. Who could blame him if he did?

Maybe you hate your life right now. Maybe you long for some dream to come true. Maybe you see no relief in sight. Don't fret. God knows the field in which you plow. And when you least expect it, you will be given the cloak of a new beginning. Whatever it is you long for, God can deliver.

Never allow yourself to fall prey to the present stench. Don't become a victim of the present. Learn from Elisha. He plowed ahead, and so must you. Press on!

The Chinese write the word crisis with two characters,
one of which means "danger" and the other "opportunity."
— *Milo Perkins*

Elisha then returned to his oxen, killed them, and
used the wood from the plow to build
a fire to roast their flesh. He passed around the
meat to the other plowmen, and they all ate.
Then he went with Elijah as his assistant.

— *1 Kings 19:21, NLT*

THIRTEEN

STICK YOUR PAST WHERE THE SUN DON'T SHINE

Elisha threw a party and invited his co-workers. They sat at the edge of a fire that devoured his plow. The wood became ash and the oxen became a meal. And they partied into the night. They laughed and reminisced about the prior years of farming. It was Elisha's way of closing the door on his past. He was a prophet now. And he never wanted to farm the back forty acres again.

Graduation means letting go of the past so you can move forward. You cannot step into the future with one leg in the past. So be as ruthless as Elisha. What are you holding onto that must be forgotten? Is it lost love? Is it the status you had in high school? Maybe you have become just one in a huge crowd of students. And you're mourning what you lost. Put it behind you. Obliterate these thoughts. There will be no going back. Put your past where the sun doesn't shine—in yesterday. Move on. It's your only option.

> The past is valuable as a guidepost,
> but dangerous if used as a hitching post.
> — *Unknown*

. . . *Many people here in this city belong to me.*

— *Acts 18:10,* NLT

FOURTEEN
How Not to Be Alone

Loneliness is a frigid moon above a bare tree. It is a train whistle at midnight. It is when we come home to an empty house, or when we hear the blues on the car radio with no one in the passenger seat. It is being single, an only child. Loneliness crosses every life, and it will cross yours. There will be times when it feels like it is raining all over the world and you are the only one getting wet, but don't let these days shape your attitude.

Always remember that there are other Christians in your city when you are feeling alone. You will need someone when loneliness creeps in. Paul did, and so will you. It is okay to feel needy. It is not a weakness to crave community. It is in our bones. We need each other. So don't retreat from the one place that tells the story of how He carried loneliness for us all.

> We are most of us very lonely in this world;
> you who have any who love you,
> cling to them and thank God.
> — *William Thackeray*

*If you find honey, eat just enough—
too much of it, and you will vomit.*

— Proverbs 25:16, NIV

FIFTEEN
How to Keep from Barfing

$\mathcal{V}$omit is not a good word. Barf is not much better. But in the Bible, it reminds us that too much can be too much. Too much of anything will make you feel like barfing. If you have too much envy, it will turn your life green with jealousy. And you will barf out the fact that you can't stand someone. Then people might not want to be around you. "All she does is run people down," they say of an envious person.

Then there is beauty. Who can ever have enough? But when too much beauty goes to your head, it will make you conceited. Who can stand a vain person? Barf!

If you find the honey of your life, don't get involved too quickly with too much emotion. Get just enough. Then see where it leads.

Always leave your options open. Don't fall in love too fast. It can make you nauseous.

> They love too much that die for love.
> — *Ancient Proverb*

$\mathcal{N}$ow there were four men with leprosy sitting at the entrance of the city gates. "Why should we sit here waiting to die?" they asked each other. "We will starve if we stay here, and we will starve if we go back into the city. So we might as well go out and surrender to the Aramean army."

— *2 Kings 7:3, NIV*

SIXTEEN
KILLING THE PAIN OF TIME

Four miserable lepers were on dead-center. Their lives were going nowhere. And one spoke up and said, "Why should we sit here waiting to die?"

It is a great question. It shows movement away from dead-center. And maybe your life has marooned. Maybe your dating life is at a dead-end street. Maybe you are living to kill the pain of time. You may be depressed with no energy, yet starved for destiny. This is dead-center.

A life that is going nowhere will develop three attitudes: helplessness, hostility, and isolation. These three make for slow death. So take back control of your life. The way to do this is to make a decision—even if it means a decision about food. Then make another one. Making small decisions will get you off dead-center. It will get your feet moving. And motion is what you need right now. Don't sit there waiting to die.

Start by doing what's necessary; then do what's possible;
and suddenly you are doing the impossible.
— *St. Francis of Assisi*

When the lepers arrived at the edge of the camp,
they went into one tent after another,
eating, drinking wine, and carrying out
silver and gold and clothing and hiding it.

— *2 Kings 7:8, NLT*

SEVENTEEN
How to Hit the Lottery

The four lepers hit the lottery! They could not believe their eyes. There was so much stuff and no one to claim it. The army was missing. The army fled when the Lord made it sound like "the clatter of speeding chariots and the galloping of horses and the sounds of a great army approaching . . ." (2 Kings 6, NLT). But it was only the grumbling stomachs of four starved lepers who could not believe their eyes. They had discovered a feast. They ate. They drank. They piled clothes up high. Maybe they were like children. Maybe they jumped into the pile. Who knows? But one thing is for certain, they made a decision. They took a baby step and it paid off. They experienced a move of God.

Our move of God can happen. All it takes is courage. And that first baby step.

> Courage consists not so much in
> avoiding danger as in conquering it.
> — *Ancient Proverb*

Then the man said, "Let me go, for it is dawn."
But Jacob panted, "I will not let you go
unless you bless me."

— *Genesis 32:26, NLT*

EIGHTEEN

GETTING A STRANGLEHOLD ON YOUR DREAMS

$\mathcal{J}$acob climbed the top rope and executed an elbow smash. A square shot to the angel's round jaw. Then Jacob picked the angel up by his golden locks. And it surprised Jacob when the angel cried, "Let me go!" But Jacob would not let go. He was "The Undertaker" with a stranglehold. And he wanted a blessing!

Blessings are a struggle. Think of Abraham. He wandered around in a tent that continually attracted sand and needed patching. Think of Noah. He knelt on the bow of the ark, hammering his eyeteeth out for a multitude of years. But, unlike Noah and Abraham, we don't fare so well. The only consistent thing about human nature is its inconsistency. Let this not be true of you. Win the battle of consistency by combining two principles—determination and hope. Don't let go until you receive your blessing!

> Do you wish to be great? Then begin by being.
> Do you desire to construct a vast and lofty fabric?
> Think first about the foundations of humility.
> The higher your structure is to be,
> the deeper must be its foundation.
> — *St. Augustine*

In time, the food became known as manna.

— *Exodus 16:31, NLT*

NINETEEN

HOW TO GO ON A LOW-FAT MONEY DIET

God seemed to be the God of a one course meal—manna. The Children of Israel had manna Pop Tarts for breakfast. Big Manna sandwiches for lunch and a manna casserole for dinner. In Egypt the Children of Israel had choices—marinated meat or fish and a choice of fruit. They no longer had the choice. No one was saying, "Do I smell hot wings?" They only complained.

We are no different. It is easy to complain when the money gets tight—and it will. Believe me. It will. Sometimes there is no money for KFC hot wings or pizza. And anytime you feel deprived, you are falling into the trap of Madison Avenue. So don't mock the goodness that God is giving you, even though it is not prime rib and lobster. Thank Him for what you do have. It will make life so much easier. Now go make that bologna sandwich with a smile.

A savage tribe is said to have no word for "Thank You."
The natives say, "Do it again."
— *Unknown*

What is the price of five sparrows?
A couple of pennies? Yet God does not
forget a single one of them.

— Luke 12:6, NLT

TWENTY

Bargain Alert! 50% Off Everything in the Store

Sparrows were a cheap source of food in Jesus' day. Who could not afford a sparrow? They were marked down from a previous markdown. Yet God did not forget them. He provided for the sparrow. And this is the beginning of a section in the Bible that is referred to as the "how much more" section. "How much more" are you worth than a half-priced source of fast food?

All of us walk around with a 50%-off tag swinging from our soul. We feel useless. We have allowed the world to price us according to beauty. And most of us feel cheaper than five sparrows. And there is a subtle message here. "Never allow the world to price you." You do not belong in the bargain bin. You have been bought with the death of God's Son. You have been redeemed. You have been priced out of this world!

> Do not lose courage in considering
> your own imperfections.
> —*St. Francis de Sales*

The eternal God is your refuge,
and His everlasting arms are under you.

— *Deuteronomy 33:27, NLT*

TWENTY-ONE

WHERE TO HIDE WHEN IT'S ALL TOO MUCH

Hide-n-seek is beneath us now.
It's a child's game.
We'd look stupid hiding in our favorite spot—
the one behind the shrubbery, the one inside the garage.
We'd be labeled psycho, in need of some help.
"He's reverted back to being a child," they'd say. But
what is wrong with that?

What would be so neurotic about playing hide-n-seek?
I'd let you be "it."
Then I'd hide too good.
For I have a place you'd never find,
and you'd have to yell, "Olly, olly, Oxen free!" And
we'd gather at home base.

Then we both could hide there. And the world?
It would never find us, in this hiding place
called Him.

> Wandering between two worlds, one dead,
> The other powerless to be born
> With nowhere yet to rest my head,
> Like these, on earth I wait forlorn.
> —*Matthew Arnold*

$\mathcal{P}$eter said, "I swear by God,
I don't know the man."
And immediately the rooster crowed.

— *Matthew 26:74, NLT*

TWENTY-TWO
KEEPING IT REAL

It was Peter's dark night of the soul, somewhere between midnight and 3 AM. Jesus was under arrest. And Peter followed the events from a safe distance—at the edge of the crowd. When he saw a bonfire, he approached it to shake off the cold. And in this place of crackling fire, some bystanders began saying to Peter, "You must be one of Jesus' disciples." Peter denied it again.

Maybe it would have been too much to explain to strangers—the sinking in the sea when he should have been walking, the last supper where bread was broken, the cutting off of a man's ear. Maybe it was just easier to deny.

Denial is the movement away from what beckons our confession. "Yes, I'm one of them. I believe in spite of my unbelief." Where do you need to confront denial? What circumstance begs for your honesty? Always remember, confession is good for the soul.

> The trouble is that everyone talks about reforming others
> and no one thinks about reforming himself.
> — *St. Peter of Alcántara*

John's disciples came to him and said, "Teacher, the man you met on the other side of the Jordan River, the one you said was the Messiah, is also baptizing people. And everybody is going over there instead of coming here to us."

— John 3:26, NLT

TWENTY-THREE
Why We're Here

$\mathcal{J}$ohn the Baptist knew his place. He was a modest man living a purpose-driven life. He knew his boundaries. But John's disciples feared losing people to the other side. They were turning baptizing into a competitive market. And business was slow on their side of the Jordan.

They burned with envy. But John viewed the other side of the Jordan as a fulfillment of the work God had appointed. He was more than willing to fold up his tent and get his waterlogged sandals and shriveled toes out of the muddy Jordan. He knew why he was here on earth. "I am here to prepare the way for Him— that is all" (John 3:28, NLT).

Make a way for Him in your family, at work or at school, and in your church. Stop envying those who have more. Quit vying for a slice of popularity. You are here to make a way for Him—that is all.

> Envy is the consuming desire to have
> everybody else as unsuccessful as you are.
> —*Frederick Buechner*

$\mathcal{B}$oaz went over and said to Ruth,
"Listen, my daughter. Stay right here
with us when you gather grain;
don't go to any other fields."

— *Ruth 2:8, NLT*

TWENTY-FOUR
YOUR UNTOLD STORY

*R*uth was a beggar and a widow with a story to tell. Her husband died in the Moabite famine, leaving her nothing but grief. She had nowhere to go and attached herself to her mother-in-law, Naomi, and they both traveled back to Israel.

On the way they met a farmer named Boaz, who everyone called Bo for short. Sure he filled his overalls nicely and liked a good chew. He was gritty with massive glands that pumped out a gallon of pure lard a day. He was no looker, but Ruth had caught his eye.

All Ruth expected to get was a meal, but she got herself a husband. And think of what might have happened if she hadn't humbled herself and received the hand of God. There would have been no marriage to Boaz. No son named Obed, who would have had no son named Jesse. And Jesse would not have had seven sons, and the seventh, David, the greatest king ever, would not have been born.

Your life has a story. God's tablet is inside.

Life: what happens to us while we are making other plans.
— *Unknown*

Always keep yourselves united in the Holy Spirit,
and bind yourselves together with peace.

— *Ephesians 4:3, NLT*

TWENTY-FIVE

TRADING SPACES: YOUR BEDROOM FOR THE DORM

*S*ometimes graduation means trading spaces—your stylish bedroom for a drab dorm. This can send you into a designing frenzy. But remember that dorm rooms are transient. For this reason, most schools will ban you from putting holes in the walls. Painting, too. If you don't like the color, put up posters. Create some type of designing distraction.

Then there is the storage issue. Dorm rooms never have enough storage. Look for ways to create storage. Put your bed on stilts and buy storage savers to put beneath.

The key is to choose a look that you and your roommate have agreed upon. Don't go off and buy things for the room without your roommate's input. This can be a relational setback. You will be sharing most everything with this person. So get started on the right foot.

Binding yourselves together by compromise will be the key when you trade spaces.

> There comes forever something between us
> and what we deem our happiness.
> — *Lord Byron*

$\mathcal{B}$ut if we look forward to
something we don't have yet,
we must wait patiently and confidently.

— *Romans 8:25, NIV*

TWENTY-SIX
How to Keep Yourself Motivated

*M*otivation is what makes us look forward. It sets our goals and thrusts us toward them. It hinges on the combination of the two principles of waiting and persevering. You wait on God to open doors while you set goals. It means you put one foot in front of the other, moving down a long, dark corridor, following the still, small voice that is His. "Your word is a lamp for my feet and a light for my path" (Psalm 119:105, NLT).

Start everyday with anticipation. Then wait with perseverance. This could be the day your dreams come true. So put on a new face and struggle against despondency. Grab hope and let go of control. Leave it in God's hands. Then wait for your spouse while dating. Work where you are while retooling for a new career. This is what it means to eagerly wait with perseverance.

The most important thing about motivation is goal setting.
You should always have a goal.
— *Francie Larrieu Smith*

I want a cabin in the woods. I'm desperate for a change from rage and stormy weather.

— *Psalm 55:8, MSG*

TWENTY-SEVEN

So You Feel Trapped—Things Will Change

So you feel trapped—things will change. The person you are in love with may not be the one you will marry. There will be other people to date. There will be other classes to ace. So take a "C" and move on. Setbacks will happen. But don't lose your smile. You are not trapped.

Life will have its shadows of disappointment. There will be times when you will want to run to the cabin in the woods. But hiding is not the answer. Don't shade your future with a shadow of despair. Because in this shadow lie the carcasses of men and women who have given up.

Always keep your options open. This will keep you aware and prepared for the next move. It will be your main goal after graduation. Learn to recognize and move with opportunities. Catching the wave of the future is your goal.

> Indeed, man wishes to be happy even when
> he so lives as to make happiness impossible.
> — *St. Augustine*

When you've stuffed yourself, you refuse dessert;
when you're starved, you could eat a horse.

— *Proverbs 27:7*, MSG

TWENTY-EIGHT
HUNGRY ENOUGH TO EAT A HORSE

*L*ife is feast or famine. Long stretches of feeling satisfied are followed by times when we could eat a horse limb by limb. But no one I know has ever eaten a horse. It is exaggeration. And exaggeration should tip us off. Something is going on here.

Anytime you exaggerate, it could mean you are losing hope. Maybe you think you will always be alone, that you will remain financially broke. For when we are famished, we exaggerate. We don't see or think straight. This is why you should never make a big decision after surgery. Never go to the grocery store when hungry. Never date when you are starving for affection. You will settle for the guy with three front teeth missing.

When you are famished, you will over look the obvious. You will settle for the wrong type of relationship. Getting involved in a relationship because you are starved for attention can result in tragedy. Don't ever go there.

Exaggeration is to paint a snake and add legs.
— *Ancient Proverb*

*J*ust as water mirrors your face,
so your face mirrors your heart.

— *Proverbs 27:19, MSG*

TWENTY-NINE

MIRROR, MIRROR ON THE WALL

*B*eauty can get your attention and strike up a pose. And after the flash, beauty cannot stand alone. It is the heart that matters. The heart can accentuate the beauty on your face. True, there are some guys who look for beauty first and follow after women for what they can get. Some are looking for a good time. They are not looking for a face that mirrors the heart. Please be aware of this. Do not think you are not beautiful because most guys choose loose morals over innocence. This has nothing to do with beauty and everything to do with lust.

Never date a guy for his looks or worry about being alone. Don't compromise. Because, in the end, you will be recognized for what is inside, and this will make all the difference. Be patient. Look into the mirror of hearts, not faces.

> Though we travel the world over to find the beautiful,
> we must carry it with us or we find it not.
> — *Ralph Waldo Emerson*

$\mathcal{I}$ was sound asleep, but in
my dreams I was wide awake.

— *Song of Songs 5:2*, MSG

THIRTY
INTERPRETING DOG DREAMS

*S*leeping dogs do dream. Their bodies shiver and shake with the fluttering of their eyes. Dogs dream about what they have experienced, like barking and running. Sometimes you can even see their paws tremble and hear faint whimpers of a bark. In their dreams, they are wide awake. Wide awake to the run they just had through the neighborhood, wide awake to some pleasant experience.

Dreaming dogs make us think. Do we have moments worth reliving in our dreams? Are we asleep or wide awake?

There is a way to occupy a life and never be fully awake. Those who make their dreams a reality take in all the stimuli. They make the risky decision and set their plans in motion. Then there are those who settle for a life of slumber. They never have a moment worth reliving. They never take a risk at all, not even in their dreams.

A dream itself is but a shadow.
—*William Shakespeare*

*I pour out my complaints before him
and tell him all my troubles.*

— *Psalm 142:2, NLT*

THIRTY-ONE

BLOGGING DOWN THE BONES

$\mathcal{B}$logs can be therapeutic, a good way to get it down. Posting your thoughts places your inner struggle on display. It puts words to those things you feel passionate about. And back before there were blogs, there were psalms.

Psalms lament and plead and worship God in the world's hearing. They were sung to some tune and felt with a beat of urgency, giving voice to the soul. Some psalms are outward expressions of an inward struggle with faith. Others are exaltations during a finer moment of life. But all are trying to communicate on a soul level. And whether you blog on the web or journal in a notebook, you will get the same impact. You will get clued in. You will discover what your soul is trying to say on a deeper level. It will feel like you are singing sweet soul music. It is a new kind of psalm. Try it. Go blogging.

Blog = weB LOG
A blog is a journal on the web.
The activity of updating a blog is "blogging" and
someone who keeps a blog is a "blogger."

$\mathcal{W}$ho is this pagan Philistine anyway, that he is allowed to defy the armies of the living God?

— *1 Samuel 17:26, NLT*

THIRTY-TWO
OVERCOMING THE FEAR THAT BINDS YOU

*G*oliath was just another thug with a rap single shooting up the charts. He stood nine feet tall and had a mouth the size of an area code. He was the father of propaganda that immobilized the Israeli camp. "I defy the armies of Israel!"

Then David, a ruddy, handsome kid, walked into the camp with a brown paper bag, dangling on his musically conditioned fingers. And he asked the one question they feared, "Who is this pagan Philistine anyway, that he is allowed to defy the armies of the living God?" (1 Samuel 17:26, NLT).

Maybe you have mapped out the route you will take through college. Maybe you have researched how to get state licensing for a trade. But you are burdened and unhappy, allowing the propaganda of fear to keep you down. It is easy to be nothing. Who wants to be that? Defy your fear! Take the next step. You have the army of the living God behind you. In the thickest part of battle, He can be found.

> Fear always springs from ignorance.
> — *Ralph Waldo Emerson*

$\mathscr{B}$ut when he looked around at the high
waves, he was terrified and began to sink.
"Save me, Lord!" he shouted.

— *Matthew 14:30, NLT*

THIRTY-THREE
MORTIFYING MOMENTS

$\mathcal{P}$eter gurgled in the foamy water, while the sun yawned into daybreak. The water was white-capping and boisterous. But it had not stopped Peter from slipping out of the boat onto the waves. Nothing is recorded about what the other disciples said. But it had to be startling to watch someone about to drown.

The fear of every life is that it might be sinking. Sometimes we get ourselves in over our heads. We procrastinate on studying. We fall in with the wrong people who live two doors down. And by the time we realize it, we are sinking into things we thought we would never do.

Please don't try to save yourself alone. Ask for forgiveness. Go talk to your professor. Seek out a trusted friend that can hold you accountable. Let someone know how you feel. And always remember who is in the troubled water with you. Reach out for His hand.

> Every time we lose courage we lose several days of our life.
> — *Maurice Maeterlinck*

In your strength I can crush an army;
with my God I can scale any wall.

— *2 Samuel 22:30, NLT*

THIRTY-FOUR
When You Hit a Wall

*W*alls are inevitable. You will hit them. And when you do, a choice has to be made. Will you scale it or will you live in its shadow? For walls have shadows. They come and go. There is even a rhythm to the shadow. It waxes and wanes. It elongates and draws in close to the wall. And there is a way to live in the shadow of the wall and never scale it. It happens when we fall into despair and defeat at its base. It happens when we stop dreaming about the future. It happens when we focus on the height of the wall, instead of scaling it.

Maybe you are living in the shadow of some daunting challenge. You can scale this wall! Never factor in the shadow or the height of the wall. To God, a wall is nothing. He can help you scale it. Don't be afraid.

> For a humble man is not afraid of failure. In fact,
> he is not afraid of anything, even of himself, since perfect
> humility implies perfect confidence in the power of God,
> before Whom no other power has any meaning and
> for Whom there is no such thing as an obstacle.
> —*Thomas Merton*

$\mathcal{D}$on't be impatient for the Lord to act!
Travel steadily along His path.

— *Psalm 37:34, NLT*

THIRTY-FIVE
DON'T GET AHEAD OF GOD

There will be times when you feel God doesn't have a plan for you. But do not get impatient. Do not get ahead of God. There is more going on behind the scenes than you realize. Timing can be the issue. God has His appointed times and His reasons for them. And the biggest mistake we can make is to get ahead of God.

Abraham and Sarah tried to outwit God. God told them to expectantly wait for a son. But Abraham and Sarah were impatient. So Sarah told Abraham to go and have a baby with one of the servant girls (Genesis 16). He did. Ishmael was born. And things were never the same. Jealousy and strife became the norm.

In what area of your life are you being impatient? Be careful. Don't get ahead of God and make your own plans happen. You will regret it the rest of your life.

> To know how to wait is the great secret of success.
> — *Xavier de Maistre*

I know how to live on almost nothing
or with everything. I have learned the secret of living
in every situation, whether it is with a full stomach
or empty, with plenty or little.

— *Philippians 4:11, NLT*

THIRTY-SIX
ATTITUDE CHECK

Paul knew circumstances in life change. They change for everyone. At times you will be lonely, at other times you will wish everyone would just leave you alone. And there will be moments of despair. Change always knocks us out of our comfort zones. This can be bad or good. It can be bad if it is caused by tragedy. It can be good if it leads us to new horizons.

So don't fight against it. Don't get caught up in "why" something has changed. Sometimes it is a question that cannot be answered. Learn to ride the wind of change. Go with it. It may lead you to a new horizon, a new job, or a new relationship. Who knows?

The key to overcoming bad circumstances is to control your attitude toward them. Be in charge of yourself. Try it. Reflect on the following prayer:

> God grant me the serenity
> to accept the things I cannot change;
> courage to change the things I can;
> and wisdom to know the difference.
> — *Reinhold Niebuhr*

I even found an altar with this inscription: *To an Unknown God.*

— *Acts 17:23, NIV*

THIRTY-SEVEN
To an Unknown God

College can breed absent-mindedness. We can get too busy for God. Then we forget Who made us and why.

Very few stop believing in God while in college. We just make Him an unknown God. We stop praying. We forget to set our alarms for church. We tell ourselves there is no benefit in worshipping God. And as one trip around the sun, turns into two, then three, then the year of graduation, we discover we don't know Him anymore. Absent-minded faith breaks the heart of God. Please don't do this. Keep your faith vibrant. Never inscribe the altar of your devotion with this inscription: To the Unknown God.

> Doubt is the disease of this inquisitive, restless age.
> — *R. Turnbull*

. . . *He* is a double-minded man, unstable in all he does.

— *James 1:8, NIV*

THIRTY-EIGHT

How to Induce Psychosis in a Rat

$\mathcal{R}$ats can go out of their minds. The way to induce psychosis is to keep changing the rules. Set up a maze. At the end, place a grain feeder to reward the rat. After a few good runs, change it up. Instead of giving the rat grain, shock him. Do it a few times, then change back to grain. The switching back and forth will drive the rat mad. This is why James says, ". . . he is a double-minded man, unstable in all he does." The switching back and forth will drive you nuts. You have to decide if you are devoted to God or not. You can't straddle the fence. You will be miserable. It will induce psychosis in your soul. So choose today. Make a clean start. You know the right thing to do. You only need to decide.

Insanity is often the logic of an accurate mind overtaxed.
— *Oliver Wendell Holmes*

*D*on't give pearls to swine!
They will trample the pearls,
then turn and attack you.

— *Matthew 7:6, NLT*

THIRTY-NINE
SWINE DIVES PROHIBITED

$\mathcal{P}$eople can be pigs. They can trample every sacred thing about you and swine dive into the middle of your business. They can sling mud too. And there will be swine in your life. There will be those who will drive you nuts. Swine love to stir the mud of gossip. They know how to be two-faced. They long to see you ostracized. They will make up lies and gossip.

The way to know if you are being influenced by swine behavior is to ask: "Is this person controlling my attitude and emotions?"

If you answered, "Yes," then the way to keep them from trampling your pearls is to confront them. You have to stand up to them. But be careful not to become emotionally volatile. When emotions get involved, you are liable to say and do things you will regret.

Do not be afraid of being honest. It can alleviate a lot of frustration. It will keep you out of their mud. And without mud, swine get disinterested.

You can't solve a problem on the same level you created it.
— *Albert Einstein*

My grief is beyond healing;
my heart is broken.

— *Jeremiah 8:18, NLT*

FORTY

What to Do When You Are Heartbroken

*L*ife is a junkyard of broken hearts. But most we never notice. They pass us on the subway and in the grocery store. They kneel beside us in the chapel and stand behind us in the café. Broken hearts can go unnoticed. Life can seep out unaware. This is why Jeremiah's groan is so important. He said it aloud and to God. He knew anguish of heart has to go somewhere. Some turn it inward upon themselves, sinking into depression. Others suffer alone. Still others try to drink it all away. It never works—this running from ourselves—it only breeds toxic self-doubt.

Jeremiah put things out in the open. He knew it would eventually help him see beyond his grief. So please go talk to someone. It will make you feel so much better. You will be able to see beyond this moment.

> Not the power to remember,
> but its very opposite, the power to forget,
> is a necessary condition for our existence.
> — *St. Basil*

Anger is cruel, and wrath is like a flood,
but who can survive
the destructiveness of jealousy?

— Proverbs 27:4, NLT

FORTY-ONE
IS IT OKAY TO BE JEALOUS?

Jealousy is a lie. It feeds you bogus information. It tells you that anyone and everyone is after what you have. It is paranoia for no reason. And if you get to the bottom of why you feel jealous, you will discover insecurity. Insecurity feeds jealousy. It is a destructiveness that cannot be survived. It is worse than anger, crueler than wrath like a flood. Jealousy never lets up. This is the evil of it. It will hammer away at self-confidence. And once you become a jealous person it is a turn off. No one can live with a jealous accuser. A jealous person will turn the inward onslaught into an outward attack. You will devour what love may be between you by this constant jealous drip.

There is no room for love when jealousy is present. "Love is not jealous or boastful or proud . . ." (1 Corinthians 13:4, NLT). You must get a grip on jealousy or it will drive away your love.

> Jealousy, the jaundice of the soul.
> — *John Dryden*

Folly delights a man who lacks judgment, but a
man of understanding keeps a straight course.

— *Proverbs 15:21, NIV*

FORTY-TWO
KEEP ON KEEPING ON

Fools lack good decision-making skills. They can't see straight. Fools make choices based upon what delights them. And if we base our choices upon what makes us feel good, we will make the wrong choice.

The way to identify foolishness is to ask yourself this question: "Am I about to do something I said I would never do again?"

Is this a relationship I said I would never get involved in again? If yes, then do not get involved.

Is this a party that I said I would never go to again? If yes, then do not go.

Is this a job that I said I would never do again? If yes, then do not take it.

Is this a fight with my family that I said I would never get involved in again? If yes, then don't.

Foolishness is doomed to repeat itself if we rush blindly into things. Stay focused. It will circumvent foolishness.

The value of life does not depend upon the place we occupy.
It depends upon the way we occupy that place.
— *St. Thérèse de Lisieux*

Come, let us tell of the Lord's greatness;
let us exalt His name together.

— *Psalm 34:3, NLT*

FORTY-THREE

WHAT TO LOOK FOR IN A RELATIONSHIP

$\mathcal{D}$ating is a game. Finding someone to marry is an art form. It is like fishing in a mud puddle—shallow and unrewarding. But do not despair. Your mate is in the world. The difficult part will be discovering his or her identity. Most look to beauty first. Then common social denominators—music, movies, love of pets, and so on. These are good, but not definitive. Something else is needed. You should be able to "exalt His name together."

Having different belief systems will complicate a relationship. So be careful not to become unequally yoked with a non-believer. He or she will convert you to limbo. Jesus called it being lukewarm. Please don't make this mistake. Know what you want in a mate. Do not compromise. Base your marriage on mutual love for God. Then you will lead a happy life, as much as one can in this fallen world.

> For a crowd is not company;
> and faces are but a gallery of pictures;
> and talk but a tinkling cymbal, where there is no love.
> — *Francis Bacon*

Give me relief from my distress . . .

— Psalm 4:1, NIV

FORTY-FOUR
STRESS EATING

$\mathcal{T}$he refrigerator has a voice. It can call to you in times of stress. It can be so ominous and relentless. So you go. You open. You lean on the door. You search the contents. The light is on. The leftover pizza from two nights ago is on the left. Behind the milk. Can you see it? There it is. Two more inches to your waistline. But who cares?

Sure, it will make you feel better when you are stressed—for a second. Then you will feel guilty. You will even hate yourself. The mirror will hate you too.

When you are stressed, do not allow food to become your safety blanket. Seek peace from God. Ask Him to give you a sign of His assurance. Seek His wisdom on how to settle a dispute. Turn to Him instead of food. But you have to be strong. Remind yourself of how you felt the last time you pigged out over stress.

Prayer is the place of refuge for every worry,
a foundation for cheerfulness, a source of constant happiness,
a protection against sadness.
— *St. John Chrysostom*

*L*et another praise you,
and not your own mouth;
someone else, and not your own lips.

—✳—

— Proverbs 27:2, NIV

FORTY-FIVE

DON'T GET STUCK ON YOURSELF

*G*etting stuck happens. We get stuck in traffic and in elevators. We are constantly trying to free ourselves from certain circumstances. Sometimes being stuck is out of our control. But being stuck on ourselves is our own fault.

The best rule is to never compliment yourself. Sure, you can have self-confidence. This attribute is admired. But there is a fine line between self-confidence and cockiness. Pride can taint even the best heart. So leave the bragging to others.

If you are insecure, work on getting self-confidence. But do not use self-praise. Ask yourself why you feel compelled to compliment yourself. Usually there is a reason. Maybe you do not feel loved. So you love yourself too much. Maybe you have never been told you are loved. Maybe you are unaware that you are idealizing yourself. If people are turned off by your attitude, you may be praising yourself too much.

> The ego is not master in its own house.
> — *Sigmund Freud*

... *Make the most of every opportunity.*

—*※—

— Colossians 4:5, NLT

FORTY-SIX

CLOSED DOORS CAN BECOME WINDOWS OF OPPORTUNITY

Eminem is wrong. Opportunity can knock more than once in a lifetime. Doors will close. This is true. But this does not mean the opportunity is gone. So what if the loan you wanted did not go through at the bank. There are other banks and lending institutions. So what if the guy you went out with last Saturday night went back to his old girlfriend. It doesn't mean you will never find love. There will be other opportunities. The trick is to not take a closed door and generalize it to all future events.

If a door closes look for an open window. Perseverance has its way of prevailing. It happened to Colonel Sanders at the age of sixty-five. He had failed at everything. His every profession was a dead-end job. Then at the age of sixty-five, he tried again. The business he started was Kentucky Fried Chicken. It was his window of opportunity.

> Opportunities are usually disguised as hard work,
> so most people don't recognize them.
> — *John James Ingalls*

If anyone has ears to hear, let him hear.

— *Mark 4:23, NIV*

FORTY-SEVEN
CAN YOU HEAR ME NOW?

*V*erizon has branded the question, "Can you hear me now?" One commercial has the Verizon man walking in snow at the North Pole. He is strolling through backwoods in another. But he is never presented where he cannot hear. And this is where Madison Avenue has us.

When Jesus said, "If anyone has ears to hear, let him hear," in a sense He was saying, "Can you hear me now?" And the presence of the question presents a problem. It opens up the possibility that we can hear and not hear. It happens on cell phones all the time. It takes us a moment to realize that the signal has dropped. We keep listening for the next word that never comes. And what Jesus is warning about is the dropped signal. The times we fail to hear Him through a friend or a spouse or a book. Ask Him to speak to you about the situation you face.

You can hear Him now.

Eyes and ears are bad witnesses to men
if they have souls that do not understand their language.
— *Heraclitus*

*M*any people say, "Who will show us better times?"
Let the smile of your face shine on us, Lord.

— *Psalm 4:6, NLT*

FORTY-EIGHT
How to Find Your Smile

The great tragedy of life is to lose our smile. Most people look for it in the things of this world. But the world cannot bring a smile. This is what the first part of this verse alludes to: "Many people say, 'Who will show us better times?' " There were those who searched for pleasure using the five senses. They were seeking a better time—another sensation greater than the last—not knowing where to find their smile.

Maybe you have lost your smile and can't seem to find it. Maybe you have been through a wilderness of frowns. Maybe you lost it in a broken relationship. Maybe you lose it everyday when you go to work. This world has a hard time producing smiles. Happiness never comes from without. It is produced by an inner faith in God. It is found in His promise, "In this world you will have trouble. But take heart! I have overcome the world" (John 16:33, NIV).

Little minds are tamed and subdued by misfortunes;
but great minds rise above them.
— *Washington Irving*

*I lie awake, lonely as
a solitary bird on the roof.*

— *Psalm 102:7, NLT*

FORTY-NINE
TAKING DOWN THE "DO NOT DISTURB" SIGN

The Psalmist has a solitary bird's-eye view of loneliness. He has put emotional distance between himself and others. And we can still do that today. We create our own loneliness by refusing to open up to new possibilities. We place a "Do Not Disturb" sign on certain emotions because we are afraid of vulnerability. We do this thinking we will avoid pain. But, in actuality, we may be pushing new opportunities away.

When we take down the "Do Not Disturb," it opens us to a new beginning.

Maybe God wants you to open up and become vulnerable. Maybe He wants you to step out like Gideon. He faced his own weaknesses. "Then the Lord turned to him and said, 'Go with the strength you have and rescue Israel from the Midianites. I am sending you!'" (Judges 6:14, NLT). God does not ask us for power, He only asks us to be willing to follow.

Take down the sign. You can do it!

Loneliness is not so much a matter of isolation as of insulation.
— *Harold W. Ruopp*

*N*ow hear my prayer; listen to my cry.
For my life is full of troubles . . .

— *Psalm 88:2-3, NLT*

FIFTY

DEALING WITH DISAPPOINTMENT

$\mathcal{D}$isappointment is in his voice, rejection too. And most would agree—life is difficult. Sometimes we shadow dance in deep recesses of doom. We feel lonely in crowds. We are agitated easily. And like the Psalmist, we feel breathless, shouting to deaf ears.

Even though the Psalmist is lamenting, his prayer is grounded in perseverance, reality, and hope. "Each day I beg for your help, O Lord; I lift my pleading hands to you for mercy" (Psalm 88:9). He released disappointment with the motion of his hands.

Disappointment will only go away if we give it permission. And sometimes it is easier to be disappointed than happy. At least we have an axe to grind. But disappointment soon turns into bitterness.

Raise your hands and release your disappointment. Now fill them with courage. It might not make you happy. But it sure helps.

Never be in a hurry; do everything quietly and in a calm spirit.
Do not lose your inner peace for anything whatsoever,
even if your whole world seems upset.
— *St. Francis de Sales*

So He went back to pray a third time,
saying the same things again. Then He came to
the disciples and said, "Still sleeping?
Still resting? Look, the time has come. . . .
Up, let's be going. See, my betrayer is here!"

— *Matthew 26:44-46, NLT*

FIFTY-ONE
MISTAKES NEED NOT BE FATAL

Jesus asked His disciples to pray. Then He found a secluded spot for His own prayers. And when He returned to check on His prayer support team, He discovered bouts of slumber. Instead of fervent prayer, He found slobber at the corners of their mouths. So, He re-commissioned them, only to find them asleep again. They were failures at praying.

Jesus could have banned them to the Garden of Gethsemane for life. He could have chained them to their own moment of failure. But Christ does not allow the past to dictate the future. He simply points out their failure, "Still sleeping? Still resting?" I like that about Jesus. I like His gentleness in the moment.

See this in your own moments of failure. Know that in your failures Christ always says, "Up, let's be going." He will always move you on away from them.

> You cannot fully claim yourself when parts of you are still
> wayward. You have to acknowledge where you are and
> affirm that place. You have to be willing
> to live your loneliness, your incompleteness . . .
> — *Henri Nouwen*

$\mathcal{T}$ake delight in the Lord, and
He will give you your heart's desires.

— *Psalm 37:4, NLT*

FIFTY-TWO

WHY YOU SHOULD THROW AWAY
THE FIRST TWO YEARS OF COLLEGE

*U*se the first two years of college to discover what comes natural to you. Try different subjects. You may discover you do not have a knack for business or marketing. You may not care about the money or idols of materialism. You may want to major in art. But get ready for the cynics. They will think it's not a good career choice. They may even say, "Major in early education. Then you can color with the kids."

Most know what they would like to do, but are afraid to venture out. We play it safe. We seek the majors that will put us on the fast track. And this seems smart, but it may lead to a mid-life crisis. So save yourself a lot of heartache. Follow your heart's desire. Get the degree in marine biology. Get the art degree and move to Greenwich Village. Major in English and minor in Theatre. Be who you were destined to be.

Do not play it safe. You are here only once.

> Progress always involves risk; you can't steal
> second base and keep your foot on first base.
>
> — *Unknown*

. . . A foolish child brings grief to a mother.

— *Proverbs 10:1, NLT*

FIFTY-THREE
MOM'S A CONTROL FREAK!

*M*om can get in your business. She wants to know every move you make. She wants to know the exact time your key turned the lock in the door last night. But understand how different life is for her. She has hovered at the window for years. She has grown accustomed to searching the darkness of the driveway for your headlight's beam. And now you are where she cannot see you. This is the problem.

Mom should kick you out of the nest. I agree. But face it. She will always feel responsible for your actions. She will feel responsible if you get a DUI. She will feel guilty when other mothers gossip about your lewd behavior. She will feel she has flunked motherhood. "A foolish child brings grief to a mother."

Remember, your mother is not trying to run your life. It is not a game to her. She only wants you to succeed. This is her motive.

> If I were hanged on the highest hill,
> Mother o' mine, O mother o' mine!
> I know whose love would follow me still,
> Mother o' mine, O mother o' mine!
> — *Rudyard Kipling*

(*Moses*) saw two Hebrew men fighting.
"What are you doing, hitting your neighbor like that?"
Moses said to the one in the wrong.
"Who do you think you are?" the man replied.
"Who appointed you to be our prince and judge?"

— Exodus 2:13-14, NLT

FIFTY-FOUR
BUTT OUT!

*W*e are nosy people. We butt in when we should keep out. Do not get in the middle of fights, even if they involve your close friends. It does not matter if it is just a verbal skirmish. Stay out of the middle. Do not try to do what Moses did. He liked being mediator of everything that was wrong with their stinking lives. It gave his life meaning. But this is the wrong motive. It will bite you in the end.

Moses learned a basic lesson. Some people live to fight. They do not want peace. And sometimes the wise thing to do is let your friends settle their own differences. Or you will become the scapegoat and their anger will turn toward you. This is what happened to Moses. So refuse to take sides. Encourage your friends to work it out. But do not become the mediator. Take it from Moses. Do not endanger your friendships.

> Do not stand in a place of danger trusting in miracles.
> — *Austrian Proverb*

Their hearts are troubled
like a wild sea in a raging storm.

— Jeremiah 49:23, NLT

FIFTY-FIVE
SOUL HURRICANES

$\mathcal{T}$he sea is a place that never stops raging, and neither will your soul. Today, somewhere beneath the layers of skin and sinew, a hurricane is brewing. Or a storm has just passed. In the eye of a soul hurricane, our emotions are battened-down beneath a sense of shock. That is why when we face the death of a loved one, we say, "I just feel numb." This is normal.

We reemerge from a soul hurricane by what Erik Erikson calls a restoring of the sense of mastery, which takes place as "we repeat, in ruminations and in endless talk . . . experiences that have been too much for us."

Sort through your emotions. Get them out. Talk on and on if you need to. This is what it takes to move on. You will need to clean up the emotional aftermath of your soul hurricane. Your future happiness depends on it.

> Emotion turning back on itself, and not leading on
> to thought or action, is the element of madness.
> — *Unknown*

In a dream, they were warned not to report back to Herod. So they worked out another route, left the territory without being seen, and returned to their own country.

— *Matthew 2:12*, MSG

FIFTY-SIX

GOD IS MORE THAN PIE-IN-THE-SKY

*H*istory would have recorded things differently if the wise men had returned to Herod. They would have forfeited their parts in our Christmas plays. There would be no *We Three Kings of Orient Are*. But they sought. They found. They worshipped. They said, "Forget Herod, that wretched man!"

Every moment of worship is met with the same problem the wise men faced. "How shall we now live?" They had to ask that question. "What shall we do with Herod? To whom shall we return?"

When we worship, we assemble to forget the wretchedness in our own soul. In worship we receive assurance. It brings light to the darkness of our nights. The same way it did the first Christmas. For even wise men have uncertainties. And maybe this is what set the wise men on their new route. Maybe they realized that God exists after all. That He is more than just some pie-in-the-sky.

> While you are proclaiming peace with your lips,
> be careful to have it even more fully in your heart.
> — *St. Francis of Assisi*

$\mathcal{M}$y head is reeling, my limbs are limp,
I'm staggering like a drunk,
seeing double from too much wine . . .

— Jeremiah 23:9, MSG

FIFTY-SEVEN
A Staggering Drunk

There are people who drink socially. Then there are those who drink to forget. They long to keep their heads reeling. So they won't have to think about their distressing lives. It is tragic. But every town has its drunk.

In my hometown, we had Spare Dime. He would walk the downtown sidewalks and hit people up for wine money. He would say, "Spare me a dime, and I will tell ya a rhyme." He was a staggering drunk.

Even though you never plan to hit bottom and beg for wine money, be careful. It only takes one stagger across the line in the highway to kill someone and yourself. Don't think that it will never happen to you. Limbs can go limp and your head can reel. This is always the danger on the open highway after a party. If you drink too much, don't drive.

Drunkenness is temporary suicide:
the happiness that it brings is merely negative,
a momentary cessation of unhappiness.
— *William Penn*

*T*hen Jesus was led by the Spirit into the desert to be tempted by the devil . . . Jesus answered, "It is written: 'Man does not live on bread alone, but on every word that comes from the mouth of God.' "

— Matthew 4:1; 4, NLT

FIFTY-EIGHT

WHAT WE CAN LEARN FROM BRAVEHEART

There is that great scene in the movie *Braveheart*, when Mel Gibson's character, William Wallace, shouts, "They may take our lives, but they will never take our freedom!" This will pump you up! But it is easy to sit in a dark theatre and cheer. It is another thing to fight a personal battle against depression or drug abuse or lust or materialism, and so on.

Speeches in movies never strengthen us for more than two hours. We cannot stand our ground by reciting mere words of a movie. But there is a power in reciting Scripture to the devil. Jesus did this. He stood His ground in the desert. He told the devil, "It is written . . ." Jesus used Scripture to help fight His own personal battles. So should we. Quote Scripture to the devil. He will eventually leave you alone. He can't stand to hear it.

One man with courage makes a majority.
— *Horace*

$\mathcal{W}$ell, you should at least have put
my money into the bank so
I could have some interest.

— *Matthew 25:27, NLT*

FIFTY-NINE
WOULDA, COULDA, SHOULDA

Everyone laments what woulda, coulda, shoulda been. There are things we would do differently. "If this woulda happened, then I coulda . . . or shoulda . . ." It's a syndrome. The servant was given the opportunity to produce results. The master said, "Take my money and make more." But the servant was lazy and only generated an excuse when the master asked for the results.

Jesus' parable is a case study on woulda/coulda/shoulda thinking. The servant missed the opportunity and regretted it later.

Remember, laziness produces a life of regret. So if you are handed an opportunity like the servant, capitalize on it. Be a go-getter. Tackle your opportunities before they become liabilities. Never leave things up for grabs. Be proactive. People notice these things. Then rewards will follow.

> For of all sad words of tongue or pen,
> the saddest are these: "It might have been!"
> — *John Greenleaf Whittier*

And God will wipe away every
tear from their eyes.

— *Revelation 7:17*, MSG

SIXTY

If Tears Were Shooting Stars

*W*hat if shooting stars are crystallized tears being thrown from heaven? What if God slings them back to earth from where they originated? Maybe He pools them in the palm of Christ's hand. Then maybe He allows Christ to shape them and throw them from some mound above the Milky Way. Could it be the sport of Heaven? Could shooting stars be crystallized tears streaking through the night?

Know that whether shooting stars are tears or not, they will be dried. There are no tears too wet for Him. No moisture when He throws them through a Van Gogh starry night.

In the morning of a new day, you will become everything you were always meant to be. And tears will never flow again. Sadness will no longer reign. So the next time you see a shooting star, maybe, just maybe, it is God drying the tears of some poor soul's eyes.

> Cry out upon the stars . . . to cross their wooing.
> — *Samuel Butler*

After the Feast was over, while His parents were
returning home, the boy Jesus stayed behind
in Jerusalem, but they were unaware of it. . .
His mother said to Him . . . "Your father and I
have been anxiously searching for you."

— *Luke 2:43; 48, NIV*

SIXTY-ONE
How Embarrassing!

It was the Passover Feast. The city was packed. People elbowed their way into the inner crust of theology. The Temple was a puddle of blood. And Mary panicked when she learned Jesus was not with Joseph. Her face flushed with embarrassment. She had lost the Son of God. But "lost" is a harsh word. It is too random, too graceless, too hopeless inside. But it was a fact. Jesus was missing.

He had been in the Temple the whole time. And Mary's heart was relieved. For three restless nights she felt those first twelve years slip away.

You will have moments of embarrassment. You will lose your own child for a moment someday—every parent does. You will have a car-wreck. You will bomb in speech class or embarrass yourself in front of some good-looking guy or girl. Embarrassment will happen. When it does, think of Mary. Her incident turned out to be not so bad. So will yours.

> When a girl ceases to blush, she has lost
> the most powerful charm of her beauty.
> — *Gregory I*

After three days they found Him in the
temple courts, sitting among the teachers,
listening to them and asking them questions.

— Luke 2:46, NIV

SIXTY-TWO
HOMESICK BLUES

In the temple, questions popped into Jesus' fertile mind. There was no mistaking. He was hungry to be with His Father. "Well, what about this? . . . What about that?" He went on for days. He loved every minute of it. It made Him forget about the homesickness He felt for His Father.

You will be homesick for awhile. It's normal. So much has changed in such a short time. Dorm rooms can seem so lonely away from the action of high school. And if you dwell on it too long, it can make you homesick. So try to keep your mind busy with the Father's business. Jesus did. He put His mind to work. So should you. Volunteer. Read a good book. Call home. Go to a movie. Do something. Just don't lie around and make yourself homesick.

Where thou art, that is Home.
— *Emily Dickinson*

So Judas threw the money into the temple and left. Then he went away and hanged himself.

— *Matthew 27:5, NIV*

SIXTY-THREE
Don't Cry over Spilt Milk

*I*n kindergarten, spilt milk was something to cry over. It was a tragic event. But no one whines in college except crybabies. You will hear them complaining to professors, to RAs, to their parents. They whine about what they don't like, about who doesn't care. And to be blunt, it's true. We don't care. We love it when they get what they deserve.

Think of Judas. What a crybaby! He cried over spilt perfume on Jesus' feet. He whined to the priests who had hired him to rat out Jesus. He begged and pleaded. He cried crocodile tears. But the priests did not care. So he threw the thirty pieces of silver back inside—five slid under the curtain, four rolled across the floor, and the rest dropped like blood.

Crybabies never get their way. So don't hate them or they will suck you in. They will have you complaining about them. Then what have you become?

A cynic can chill and dishearten with a single word.
— *Ralph Waldo Emerson*

$\mathcal{B}$ut I tell you that anyone who looks at a woman lustfully has already committed adultery with her in his heart.

— *Matthew 5:28, NIV*

SIXTY-FOUR
DIRTY LITTLE THOUGHTS

$\mathcal{T}$houghts happen. You can be walking on campus or driving in your car. You can be sitting in class when they walk by. And before you know it, you have zeroed in. It is hard not to look when they strut their stuff. They look so fine.

Jesus knew hot-blooded men will lust. But what shocks about this verse is the indictment of "looking." Everybody looks. So does that mean everybody commits adultery with their eyes?

The difference between a dirty thought and a beautiful one is what you do with it. Having a beautiful thought is not a sin. God made beauty and we recognize it. But if you take that thought to the next level and think, "I wish I could . . ." Then you have crossed over into lust. Lust happens when we change a beautiful thought into a dirty little wish.

> Before a man gives way to his passions,
> even if his thoughts mount an assault against him,
> he is always a free man in his own city and
> he has God as an ally.
> — *St. Dorotheos of Gaza*

$\mathcal{Q}$uick! Catch all the little foxes before
they ruin the vineyard of your love . . .

—※—

— *Song of Solomon 2:15, NLT*

SIXTY-FIVE

TOP FIVE RELATIONSHIP FIXERS

1. Let each other have ten uninterrupted minutes to talk.

— *Job 33:1*

2. Agree to stop trying to fix each other.

— *Genesis 13:8*

3. Go on a real date. Act like it's your first.

— *Song of Solomon 2:14*

4. Don't have unrealistic standards.

— *Romans 3:23*

5. Don't disqualify the positive. Look for both—good and bad.

— *Song of Solomon 2:8*

I cannot love as I have loved,
And yet I know not why;
It is the one great woe of life
To feel all feeling die.
— *Philip James Bailey*

Smooth words may hide a wicked heart,
just as a pretty glaze covers a common clay pot.

— *Proverbs 26:23, NLT*

SIXTY-SIX
WHAT COVERGIRL CAN'T COVER

*M*akeup is good. It can cover blemishes and accentuate your positives. But CoverGirl cannot conceal what you feel inside. It can't cover low self-esteem. And there are people who prey on those with no self-worth. They know how to smooth talk. They know how to build you up, how to talk you into doing things.

"Come on what's wrong with you," they say.

Being pressured into doing things is not an innocent relationship. You need to know what they are really after. It could be a booty call. And this is when you have to be courageous. If you base self-worth on being liked and popular, you will give in. Then you will hate yourself when they move on the following day. Be your own person. Have the guts to say, "I don't think so." This will build self-confidence. And smooth talkers will go by the wayside.

> He that respects himself is safe from others;
> He wears a coat of mail that none can pierce.
> — *Henry Wadsworth Longfellow*

An empty stable stays clean,
but no income comes from an empty stable.

— *Proverbs 14:4, NLT*

SIXTY-SEVEN
Enduring the Job That Stinks

*M*ost people would rather be unemployed than shovel muck. Their pride will not allow them to stoop and scoop and scrape and smell the remains of the day. And if the proverb is saying anything, then it is saying that there is a way to loaf and there is a way to pay your bills. Who doesn't want to loaf? Who doesn't want to hit the road like Jack Kerouac and bop to San Francisco? It beats cleaning out a stable, and even though freeloading is good for a season, it doesn't pay the bills over the long haul.

You are a graduate now, and graduates start out having to perform jobs that will be below them. Everyone has a job that stinks in one way or the other. But stay at it because: "Lazy people want much but get little, but those who work hard will prosper and be satisfied" (Proverbs 13:4, NLT).

> Even if money did grow on trees,
> some people wouldn't shake a limb to get it.
> —*Your Parents*

So Jezebel sent this message to Elijah:
"May the gods also kill me if by this time
tomorrow I have failed to take your life
like those whom you killed."

— *1 Kings 19:2, NLT*

SIXTY-EIGHT
How to Deal with a Drama Queen

Queen Jezebel was a drama queen. She tried to get Elijah caught up in her emotions. She was enraged about the showdown on Mount Carmel. Her prophets were dead, and she was no longer the center of attention and power. So she threatened to kill Elijah. And he fell for the drama and ran. He collapsed into a deep depression under a broom tree and wanted to die.

Drama queens want the spotlight. And they will do whatever it takes to get it. But do not fall for their performance. They want you to become emotionally involved. It takes away the logic. Elijah had no reason to fear. He had just defeated the prophets of Baal. But he was unable to remove himself from Jezebel's emotions.

Never allow someone to take away logic. You will need both logic and emotions when facing a difficulty. Think things through before you act.

> Behavior is a mirror in which
> every one displays his image.
> — *Goethe*

*Joshua and the Israelite army fled toward
the wilderness as though they were badly beaten, and all the
men in the city were called out to chase after them.
In this way, they were lured away from the city.*

— *Joshua 8:15-16, NLT*

SIXTY-NINE
DON'T GET CAUGHT WITH YOUR PANTS DOWN

Every great defensive end in football knows how to stay home. They are not tricked by a reverse. And Joshua ran a reverse play! He devised a great battle plan. He used mob psychology. He led the entire city astray. Joshua said, "When I say run, hightail it. And when they chase us, we will send in an army behind us." And the inhabitants of the city took the bait.

Then they realized that they had been had. And their city was in flames. They had fallen for the oldest trick in the playbook.

Mob psychology is a weird phenomenon. Beware of it. It happens when we follow the crowd and not moral standards. Do not let yourself be fooled. The "everybody is doing it" thinking will be at every party and function. Keep to your standards. Be individualistic. Follow the beat of your own drummer. Then you will not get caught with your pants down.

> …Those who wish to live virtuously should not hanker after
> praise, be involved with too many people, keep going out,
> or abuse others (however much they deserve it), or talk
> excessively, even if they can speak well on every subject.
> — St. Diadochos of Photiki

One day Ahaziah fell through
the balcony railing on the rooftop of his
house in Samaria and was injured.

— *2 Kings 1:2, MSG*

SEVENTY
The Famous Last Words of a Redneck: "Watch This!"

The Consumer Product Safety Commission reports that the five most dangerous household accidents are: stairs, glass doors, cutlery, glass bottles and jars, and home power tools. Even though Ahaziah's accident is not in the top five, it happened. Maybe he threw a party. Maybe the band was thumping and the wine was flowing. Maybe he yelled, "Watch this!" Then he leaned over the balcony railing to pour wine on guests below. Who knows? But there are the rednecks, the brave ones, the crazy ones, the fraternity nuts who do stupid stuff for attention.

Don't try dim-witted stunts. Don't play the fool. Think before you taunt death from the edge of some balcony. Your life is more precious than winning some bet. Hazing is not how you want to become part of a group.

Accidents will happen. So please think before you act. Remember logic. We don't want to lose you.

> If Stupidity got us into this mess,
> then why can't it get us out?
> — *Alexander Pope*

A man with leprosy came and knelt before him and said,
"Lord, if you are willing, you can make me clean."
Jesus reached out His hand and touched the man.
"I am willing," He said. "Be clean!"
Immediately he was cured of his leprosy.

— *Matthew 8:2-3, NIV*

SEVENTY-ONE
PLAYING JESUS TO THE LEPERS IN YOUR HEAD

$\mathcal{L}$eprosy is an unclean condition. It is erosion of the skin. And there is leprosy of the mind—unclean thinking. Leprous thoughts are neurotic thoughts that condemn us for not being perfect. It can happen when we feel we are not good enough to receive our parent's approval.

"If they were proud of you, they would tell you. You are a disappointing child." These are leprous thoughts. They make us feel broken and unclean inside.

You may have a parent who never gives you their approval. You must come to terms with this. Stop trying to be perfect to win them. This is, as U2 puts it, playing Jesus to the lepers in your head. You will never cast out every tidbit of imperfection or do enough to get their vocal endorsement. So relax. Stop trying to be a god. Understand that your parents may not know how to give approval. Maybe their parents never gave it to them.

Every man has his own destiny:
the only imperative is to follow it, to accept it,
no matter where it leads him.
— Henry Miller

. . . If you put away the sin that is in your hand and allow no evil to dwell in your tent, then you will lift up your face without shame; you will stand firm and without fear.

— *Job 11:15, NIV*

SEVENTY-TWO
FACING SHAME

$\mathcal{T}$he basics in Junior High: note writing, writing on your hands, instant messaging, all-night phone conversations, your parents chauffeuring you around. Now you are far removed from the simple life. Innocence is gone. A battle rages. There is darkness where there once was light. Shame where there once was innocence. But innocence can be restored. You can update this basic.

Job was unable to raise his head. He was loaded down with shame. He could not look God in the eyes. This is the death of innocence. Shame is a result of sin. And when we sin, the last thing we want to do is face our God. We do not want to pray or read our Bible. Church becomes a place where we have to do business with our sins. So we stay away. But the way to "brighten in innocence" is to face the reasons for our shame. Seek forgiveness.

> The truly innocent are those who not only are
> guiltless themselves, but who think others are.
> — *Josh Billings*

$\mathcal{W}$e don't play the major role.
If we did, we'd probably go around
bragging that we'd done the whole thing!

— *Ephesians 2:9, MSG*

SEVENTY-THREE

LIVING IN THE PAPARAZZI'S SHUTTER

*L*ife is a never ending search for bragging rights. We brag with our clothes. We strut in our shoes. We cruise in our cars. We want to be seen. We want the attention, the accolades. We want to "play the major role." We want to live in the shutter of the paparazzi. Or at least look and act like we are. But the lesser role is better. It is much simpler. You will not go broke trying to keep ahead of the pack. You will not be exhausted either.

We have to decide which role we are willing to play. Jesus played the lesser one. "Think of yourselves the way Christ Jesus thought of Himself. He had equal status with God but did not think so much of Himself that He had to cling to the advantages of that status no matter what. Not at all" (Philippians 2:5-7, MSG).

Go and do likewise.

> Humility must accompany all our actions, must be with us
> everywhere; for as soon as we glory in our good works
> they are of no further value to our advancement in virtue.
> — *St. Augustine*

Simon Peter announced, "I'm going fishing."
The rest of them replied, "We're going with you."
They went out and got in the boat.
They caught nothing that night. . . .
(Jesus) said, "Throw the net off the right side
of the boat and see what happens."

— John 21:3; 6, MSG

SEVENTY-FOUR

FISHING FOR A DATE, NOT A LOVER

Fishing is a way of life. We fish for respect, for compliments, for somebody to date. And dating can come down to where you drop your line. If you are fishing for a date, don't drop your line at the local bingo spot. You might get a supercharged Viagra freak. If you fish at a frat party, you won't even get a bite. Artificial bait and loose morals work well in some places.

So ask yourself: What type of person am I fishing for? The answer will determine where you drop the line. And it may be a place you have not thought of. Your true love may be in deeper water. You may not meet them for two more years. Who knows? But if you are not catching anything, maybe it is time to follow Christ's advice. Peter did. He fished on the other side of the boat. Try a new spot. See what happens.

What is a date, really, but a job interview that lasts all night?
— *Jerry Seinfeld*

I say this as bluntly as I can to wake you up to the stupidity of what you're doing. Is it possible that there isn't one levelheaded person among you who can make fair decisions when disagreements and disputes come up?

— *1 Corinthians 6:5, MSG*

SEVENTY-FIVE

TAKING SIDES IN PARENTAL DISAGREEMENTS

The sad answer to Paul's question is still "no." We are still not levelheaded. We are a fractured society. The divorce rate is fifty percent. And the sin of every divorced parent is the feud they start with their ex. The venom is vicious. The fight is personal. Then it spews into your life, forcing you to choose sides.

You do not have to take a side. Remember that your father will always be your father. Your mother is still the one who gave birth to you. There is no such thing as a side. Not to you. Try to remain neutral. Your survival tactic will be to head off their tirades. Tell them you are not having this conversation. Say you will come back later or call back when they have something different to talk about. Keep a solid front. They will succumb to defeat. When misery does not get company, it moves on.

> The difference between the right word and
> the almost right word is the difference between
> lightning and the lightning bug.
> — *Mark Twain*

$\mathcal{B}$ut whether or not their motives are pure,
the fact remains that the message about
Christ is being preached, so I rejoice.
And I will continue to rejoice.

— *Philippians 1:18, NLT*

SEVENTY-SIX
As Seen on Religious Television

I see them when I run the channels—the loud mouths, the religious fervor. Can you believe that wig? Have you ever seen such gaudy furniture? What is the message anyway? I've lost it. It happened the third time through the channels. Nothing was on—MTV, CMT, CNN, The Weather Channel—then the religious one.

I stop.

I wanted to hear. Then my phone rang. It was a woman. Her voice was a low murmur. She said she had been watching the channel—the one I can't stand. She said she had been trying to hang on. The channel helped her. And somehow, through the spittle and the heated-breath of the airwaves, she had heard. And I had heard too. This station may be their only help. Sometimes it is the only hope they hear and receive.

I know this now, because she called and told me. Then she asked, "Will you pray with me, Pastor?"

> Christianity has not been tried and found wanting.
> It has been found difficult and left untried.
> — G. K. *Chesterton*

About the ninth hour Jesus cried out in a loud voice,
"Eloi, Eloi, lama sabachthani?" —which means,
"My God, my God, why have you forsaken me?"

— *Matthew 27:46, NIV*

SEVENTY-SEVEN
WHY GOD WILL NEVER TURN HIS BACK ON YOU

In the moment when God, the Father, should have been present, He was absent. On a day when an earthly father could have consoled, Joseph was missing. Both fathers, earthly and Heavenly, were not present in Christ's darkest hour. Joseph had, by most accounts, died by the time Jesus was crucified. And His Heavenly Father turned His back in this hour. He had to. This was His Son in Whom He was well-pleased. But Christ had to suffer indelible rejection to set us free.

Maybe your father was not present at graduation. Maybe you, like Jesus, buried your earthly father. Now you cannot look out to see his face. Know, as much as it is possible to know, your father is proud of you. He would have been at your graduation if he only understood. So when you feel alone, think of Christ. When you see other people enjoying their fathers, think of Christ. He endured the Cross so you would never know what it would feel like to lose both.

He who has once placed his hope in God no longer is
concerned over himself, and in whatever he does,
in everything, he will find profit for his soul.
—*St. Paisius Velichkovsky*

$\mathscr{S}$amson went down to Timnah with his father and
mother. When he got to the vineyards of Timnah,
a young lion came at him, roaring. The Spirit of God
came on him powerfully and he ripped it open
barehanded, like tearing a young goat.

— Judges 14:5-6, MSG

SEVENTY-EIGHT
You Can Whip This Class without No-Doz

In a blinding flash, the lion roared at Samson. He had no choice but to respond. He ripped it apart barehanded. It was a bloody mess. Sinew and bones exposed. Then he stood over it and stared. He was panting. Sweat like blood drops poured from his face. He had defeated a lion!

You will have classes that roar at you like a lion. They will be tough. Courageous strength will be needed for some classes. You will work harder for the same grade. It will be a struggle. You will even find yourself tempted by uppers. But you can whip this class. You have what it takes to defeat this lion. Samson had supernatural strength. The Spirit of God came on him. Pray for God to come on you. Tell Him you need Samson-like strength. Ask Him to give you the supernatural ability to complete the work. He will. Don't depend on No-Doz. There is another power.

I am tied to the stake, and I must stand the course.
— *William Shakespeare*

*S*ome time later, when (Samson) went back to
marry her, he turned aside to look at the
lion's carcass. In it was a swarm of bees and
some honey, which he scooped out with
his hands and ate as he went along.

— *Judges 14:8-9, NIV*

SEVENTY-NINE
FINDING YOUR HONEY AND EATING IT TOO

*W*hat a pleasant surprise—honey where only maggots eat! The carcass of the lion that was by now rotten contained a delicacy. Inside the rib cage, beneath the chest cavity was the sweetest honey you ever could eat. It turned Samson into Winnie the Pooh.

One of the curiosities of this passage is why Samson detoured. Who would want to see what the maggots had eaten? So this is strange behavior. Unless we understand, everyone needs to relive victories. And the thing to notice is the way he savored the moment. He scooped up the honey. He enjoyed the sweetness of victory.

There are victories in life you should revisit. Go scoop up the honey. It might be just the thing you need at this moment. Think back to one of your sweetest memories. Bring it to mind. Mull it over. It will help you see that life hasn't been all bad.

> What we obtain too cheap, we esteem too lightly;
> it is dearness only that gives everything its value.
> — *Thomas Paine*

The moment I decide to do good,
sin is there to trip me up.

— *Romans 7:21, MSG*

EIGHTY
Never Thin Enough

Some girls are too thin. But they can't seem to see it in the mirror. So they work harder to be thinner. They eat less. They starve themselves to look like the model—the one on the cover of the magazine. But good health must be your priority.

And it is no longer just a female issue. Guys want what they see in music videos and magazines too. The emergence of shirtless pop stars and rappers is driving this craze. Guys want a great upper body. And they will go to extremes to get it. Some even shoot steroids. They are looking for an instant payoff and are forgetting long-term health.

Please be wise about having a great-looking body. We all want one. But don't kill yourself trying. No one looks good in a casket.

Fact: Between 5-20% of individuals
struggling with anorexia nervosa will die.
— *www.NationalEatingDisorders.org*

The Lord replied, "Is it right for you
to be angry about this?"

— *Jonah 4:4, NLT*

EIGHTY-ONE
KICKING THE DOG

*G*od was helping Jonah do a gut check. Did he have the right to be angry? There are times when we should lose our temper. Injustice is one. Stupidity that gets others hurt is another. But being angry at the wrong person is not okay. It is called "displaced anger." It is taking out our anger on innocent bystanders.

It happens when we get angry at our boss and on the way home when we give the driver in front of us hand signals. It happens when we kick the dog because we are mad at our girlfriend. Displaced anger makes us look like a fool in front of our friends. They will say, "What's wrong with him?" Anger is not always a bad thing. But when it is uncalled for, it is wrong. Be honest with your anger. Ask yourself before you get angry if it's worth it. Don't direct your anger at the wrong person.

Anger dwells only in the bosom of fools.
— *John Dryden*

$\mathcal{T}$hen he said to his young servant,
"On your feet now! Look toward the sea."
He went, looked, and reported back, "I don't see a thing."
"Keep looking," said Elijah, "seven times if necessary."

— *1 Kings 18:43*, MSG

EIGHTY-TWO
WHAT'S ON YOUR HORIZON?

Elijah was looking for rain. He needed rain. The nation needed rain. The drought was in its third year. And when Elijah sent his servant to look for rain, there was not a cloud in the sky. And the servant reported back, "I don't see a thing."

"Keep looking, seven times if necessary."

Elijah was not looking for rain. He was looking for a sign of coming rain. There is a huge difference. One is the big picture. The other looks for the steps it takes to get there.

What small step do you see? Will this step take you to the new career, the new opportunity on your horizon? For Elijah it was a fist-sized cloud. So look for the cloud. The cloud could be an internship. It is anything that will look good on your resume. Paid or volunteer. This is how you will reach your horizon. Look for clouds, not rain.

> The present is big with the future.
> — *Rudyard Kipling*

$\mathcal{T}$hings happened fast. The sky grew black
with wind-driven clouds, and then a
huge cloudburst of rain, with Ahab
hightailing it in his chariot for Jezreel.

— 1 Kings 18:45, MSG

EIGHTY-THREE
DON'T WISH YOUR LIFE AWAY

*L*ife creeps along. Sometimes we feel like the inchworm trying to get to the ark. It seems as if we will never get to the place of safety, the voyage above the waves. Then on a dime, life can turn fast and furious. Three years can become a blur. Things can happen fast. The drought was over in a matter of minutes. The bottom fell out. It rained like cats and dogs.

Let it be a reminder. Your drought can be over quickly. You will find the job. You will meet the person you will marry. Graduation will come again. This time it may be your last time to walk the line. Things can happen fast. So don't wish your life away while you wait. Stay present in the moment. Check your timing. This may not be the right time. Be patient. The bottom will fall out one day. The drought will be over.

> In three words I can sum up everything
> I've learned about life: it goes on.
> — *Robert Frost*

O Lord, God of my salvation, I have
cried out to you day and night. Now hear
my prayer; listen to my cry.

— *Psalm 88:1-2, NLT*

EIGHTY-FOUR
FINDING THE END OF OURSELVES

The Psalmist's voice was weak from crying. He needed God's attention but received silence. And it's puzzling. Who understands the silence of God? But sometimes God doesn't answer us because we are whining. And maybe God wouldn't let the Psalmist get his way. Who knows? Sometimes we have a tendency to gripe. We whine to God like a child does to a parent. And sometimes God lets us cry as mothers let their children cry.

Mothers know that sometimes crying will soon turn into sleeping. And if not for the crying the sleeping would not come. If not for the silence of God, we would never find the end of ourselves—that moment when we let go and give God control, that moment when we find our own child-like rest.

The end of self is not a bad place to be. If you are there, let go. Get some rest.

> When we want to be something other than the thing
> God wants us to be, we must be wanting
> what, in fact, will not make us happy.
> — C.S. *Lewis*

$\mathcal{T}$he king and all the people with him
arrived at their destination exhausted.
And there he refreshed himself.

— *2 Samuel 16:14, NIV*

EIGHTY-FIVE
CALIFORNIA OR BUST!

*S*ummertime means vacation time. It means traveling toward a destination: "California or Bust!" And no flat tire or overheated radiator has ever stopped a vacation. Circumstances have delayed us, but most of the time we keep traveling.

David's men were tattered and ragged. But they did not stop until they reached their destination. And the destination soothed their weary feet. It massaged away the exhaustion. They discovered rest.

You will know fatigue after graduation. You will feel rundown. But don't stop. Stay resolved to reach your destiny. And one way to stay resolute is to write down your destination point. It could be college, or attending a tech school, or finding the right sales job. Whatever it is, write it in the blank below. It will get you started toward your destination. And remember refreshment takes place when you get there. There is nothing like making a decision, and then realizing the fruit of it.

"_____ OR BUST!"

He that can take rest is greater than he that can take cities.
— *Benjamin Franklin*

It's best to stay in touch with both sides of an issue. A person who fears God deals responsibly with all of reality, not just a piece of it.

— *Ecclesiastes 7:18, MSG*

EIGHTY-SIX
WHAT YOU CAN LEARN FROM JACK AND JILL

Jack and Jill went up the hill to fetch bottled water. Jack fell down. He broke both arms and busted his crown. And Jill came tumbling after. Now Jack has been out of work for a year. And Jill wonders: Will he ever work again? Will he ever be able to bring home bottled water?

Jill never bargained for sickness. She wanted to marry Jack and live happily ever after. But reality took a bite out of old-fashioned love. The idea of living happily ever after was crushed on the hill. Bones and marrow can dictate the heart. Jill discovered this.

Be a realist. Love is not infatuation. Believe in the marriage vow, "in sickness and in health." You may greet both. So take a moment and think about the person you may be in love with. Could you love this person in sickness and in health?

> This sickness doth infect
> the very lifeblood of our enterprise.
> — *William Shakespeare*

The king of Israel answered Jehoshaphat, "There is still
one man through whom we can inquire of the Lord,
but I hate him because he never prophesies anything good
about me, but always bad. He is Micaiah son of Imlah."

— *1 Kings 22:8, NIV*

EIGHTY-SEVEN
FIND SOMEONE WHO CAN TELL YOU THE TRUTH

*T*ruth is hard to find. And Ahab and Jehoshaphat needed truth. They were trying to decide on war. Syria was the enemy, a wretched bunch. And the king's advisors said, "Yes. Go!" But Jehoshaphat wanted to inquire of the Lord. He needed a prophet. And Ahab said, "There's this one prophet who might be able to help. But I hate his guts. He never says anything good about me."

Jehoshaphat replied, "That's just the guy we need."

Jehoshaphat wanted truth, the kind Ahab refused. And you will have friends who will never tell you the truth. Not that they are trying to lie. It may not be in their personality to give you the pros and cons. They do not want to hurt your feelings.

Cultivate friends who can help you see both sides of a situation. They will use truth to guide you, not tear you down.

Then comes the hard part—the courage to listen.

> How sweet the words of Truth,
> breath'd from the lips of Love.
> — *James Beattie*

So He bent over her and rebuked the fever, and it left her. She got up at once and began to wait on them.

— *Luke 4:39, NIV*

EIGHTY-EIGHT
GETTING BACK TO NORMAL

$\mathcal{H}$ere is a woman who had her life interrupted by sickness. And after being healed, she returned to her daily chores. She did not start a healing ministry. She did not hock holy water from the Jordan. She simply made a meal.

Maybe you have endured an illness, or a breakup in a relationship, or you are suffering from the blues of having graduated. Whatever the malady, the key to moving beyond the moment is to reestablish a routine. You can do this by not skipping meals. Eat something. Get back on your exercise program. It will send a signal to your body that things are returning to normal. Schedule set times in your day to accomplish a task—any task. Then do it religiously. It will re-center your mind.

Don't let highs become highs and lows become lows. Remain levelheaded. And a routine will aid you. It will give your mind and body something to concentrate on, instead of worrying.

As a cure for worrying, work is better than whiskey.
— *Ralph Waldo Emerson*

A leech has twin daughters named
"Gimme" and "Gimme more."

—※—

— *Proverbs 30:15*, MSG

EIGHTY-NINE
WHAT YOUR PARENTS NEVER WANT YOU TO KNOW

$\mathcal{T}$he leech is never satisfied with a value meal. It always wants to super-size. It wants to trade in the Ford Taurus for a BMW. Who wouldn't? But not everyone can afford to upgrade. You might be someone who cannot afford to dress in designer clothes or drive a Mercedes. You may have little money and no Kate Spade bag to carry it in. That is okay. Just don't feel deprived. Your parents may be sacrificing more than you realize. But they would never tell you. They do not want you to feel like a burden. So do not dishonor them by feeling disadvantaged. Be thankful. They need to know that their sacrifice is making a difference in your life.

No one can stand a leech that cries and complains for more when all is being given. Take your parents feelings into consideration. Please do not burden them. They have feelings. Leeches do not. They are forever crying for more.

We never know the love of the parent till
we become parents ourselves.
—*Henry Ward Beecher*

---

*L*ook up at the sky. Take a long hard look.
See those clouds towering above you?

— *Job 35:5*, MSG

NINETY
LIFE ON CLOUD 9

*T*here is no rain on Cloud 9. There is nothing there to depress you. Cloud 9 is a perfect place of bliss. There is plenty of sunshine. You lack nothing on Cloud 9. But no one lives above the clouds, much less aboard one. And below the clouds it rains. Poverty exists. Acne erupts. There is pain in childbirth. Being dumped on happens below the clouds. And when you are beneath something, the way to rise above it is to protect yourself. Do not get dumped on. Buy a couple of umbrellas. Don't feed sea gulls on the beach. Why? Because they will drop on you, that's why. And the same goes with people. Don't let them dump on you. Don't subject yourself to their manipulative ways. Stop feeding them your love. If they dump on you once, they will do it again. You are not living on Cloud 9.

> Why should I cherish in my heart a hope that devours me—
> the hope for perfect happiness in this life—
> when such hope, doomed to frustration,
> is nothing but despair.
> —*Thomas Merton*

*J*abez prayed to the God of Israel: "Bless me,
O bless me! Give me land, large tracts of land.
And provide your personal protection—
don't let evil hurt me." God gave him what he asked.

— 1 Chronicles 4:10, MSG

NINETY-ONE
WHY THE PRAYER OF JABEZ MAY CAUSE HAIR LOSS

*J*abez prayed for more land. That is not so good. Don't get me wrong. Land is good. But more land? Who wants the responsibility of it? Imagine owning Manhattan. Donald Trump is losing his hair over maintaining a tower downtown. So don't think owning more land is better. It may have been good for Jabez. But that might not translate to us.

The Bible does not record what happened after Jabez's tracts of land increased. What the Bible traces is Solomon's meaningless pursuit of riches. "Yet when I surveyed all that my hands had done and what I had toiled to achieve, everything was meaningless, a chasing after the wind; nothing was gained under the sun" (Ecclesiastes 2:11, MSG). Do not pray for more land in this world. It will only mean more headaches and responsibility. Learn to expand the boundaries of the Kingdom of God. Leave the towers to Donald Trump.

> We are here on earth to do good to others.
> What the others are here for, I do not know.
> — *Matthew Arnold*

You ou looked at me, and I fell in love.
One look my way and I was hopelessly in love!

— *Song of Solomon 4:9, MSG*

NINETY-TWO
LONG-DISTANCE RELATIONSHIPS

*Y*ou know what people say about long-distance relationships: "They never work out." But you may think you can beat the odds. There is nothing wrong with that. But there are negatives in this type of relationship.

You will never actually touch this person. This can be good and bad. It can be good if you are sexually attracted more than you should be. It can be bad if your relationship has been built on physical attraction. Body chemistry will no longer play a role. The relationship will have to survive on other elements. Talking on the phone is the number one way of keeping the relationship thriving. And the one thing a long-distance relationship will reveal is what brought you together. If fighting is all you do now, then it may mean that you never really knew this person outside a physical attraction. If this is true, you will not beat the odds.

> Real happiness is cheap enough,
> yet how dearly we pay for its counterfeit.
> — *Hosea Ballou*

Show us how much you love us, God!
Give us the salvation we need!

— *Psalm 85:7, MSG*

NINETY-THREE
THE CINDERELLA SYNDROME

Chances are you have a step-parent. Most everyone does these days. And hopefully, you are not being treated like Cinderella. She had to work harder to stay in her step-mother's graces, and even then she was treated horribly. And in some small way being a step-child gives us the Cinderella syndrome. We can feel deprived of the same love and attention given to step-siblings.

Even though you may never achieve unconditional love from your step-parents, it will not change your future. Be the same considerate person you have always been. Cinderella did not change her personality when the fairy changed her status. And in the end, she got the prince. She was delivered from that wicked household. So remember that you are looking for the prince or princess, not unconditional love from a step-parent. Don't become so bitter over your parent's divorce that you miss the ball. God will show you His love by providing the salvation you need.

> Still achieving, still pursuing,
> Learn to labor and to wait.
> — *Henry Wadsworth Longfellow*

*B*ut they were no sooner out to sea than a
gale-force wind, the infamous nor'easter, struck.
They lost all control of the ship.
It was a cork in the storm.

— *Acts 27:14*, MSG

NINETY-FOUR
A Shipwreck on the Sheets

$\mathscr{S}$hipwrecks happen. They happen at sea. They take place on the sheets of your bed after a breakup. Crying floods the stream of love you once had in your heart. The rudder has been torn away. You become a cork in the storm. And you drift from the life that you thought would be yours. Shipwrecks happen. We can be thrown off balance by an unexpected occurrence. And the key to life is to learn to wax and wane with circumstances, to flex but not bend, to drift but not become marooned.

Ride out the storm. We do this by battening down the hatches—those places where unwanted emotions can rush in. Do not frequent the places where you will encounter your ex. Take down the pictures. Hope for the sunshine. Look for the rainbow. Establish a new rudder that will steer you clear of old emotions. Your ship will sail again.

A little gale will soon disperse that cloud.
And blow it to the source from whence it came.
— *William Shakespeare*

You know that I had the kingdom right in my hands and everyone expected me to be king, and then the whole thing backfired and the kingdom landed in my brother's lap—God's doing.

— *1 Kings 2:15, MSG*

NINETY-FIVE
THE THINGS THAT DROP IN YOUR LAP

*N*othing falls in your lap. Adonijah should have known this. But he was bitter. He thought the kingdom belonged to him instead of Solomon. He believed that God dropped it in Solomon's lap. But nothing gets dropped. Most things get earned. And you will have to earn something after graduation. It may be money, a degree, or a spouse. It doesn't matter. Decisions will have to be made. You will have to sacrifice now to reap the reward later. Reaping and sowing is a law of the universe. And if you can start analyzing what you are sowing, then you can control what you reap. Sow into a degree and get—hopefully—a better job. Spend a lot of time in the dating scene and you will reap a spouse. Nothing will simply drop in your lap. You will have to work for most everything you get.

> Happiness is a choice that requires effort at times.
> — *Aeschylus*

$\mathcal{T}$ime to get up, God—get moving.

—*※*—

— *Psalm 10:12, MSG*

NINETY-SIX
WAKE-UP CALL #49

*W*hat boldness! The Psalmist has the nerve to give God a wake-up call. He wanted God to get moving, as if God were slumbering. And you have had a lifetime of wake-up calls. But they are over. After graduation it is just you and the alarm clock. That's it. No one will knock on your door. Your parents will not pull you out of bed. No wake-up call from the front desk. You are the master of your domain. But the domain is still in a time zone. This is the bummer. So make it a habit to get up. Then get to class on time. This will do two things for you: 1) You will feel prepared, which will boost confidence. 2) It will reduce stress. Running late can heighten your stress level. It can make you spill your coffee too. That's not good—you will need every drop. So remember that time has to be managed, not forgotten.

You may delay, but time will not.
— *Benjamin Franklin*

$\mathcal{H}$e gave them exactly what they asked for—
but along with it they got an empty heart.

— *Psalm 106:15*, MSG

NINETY-SEVEN
GETTING WHAT YOU WANT

*G*od is not a genie-in-a-bottle. You cannot rub out of Him three wishes. But if you really think you know what is best for you, He will grant your wishes. Just cry and beg and tell Him you will die if you do not get it. It worked for the Children of Israel. They accused God of carrying them into the desert to kill them. Now of course, He did not. But they would not shut up. They complained about everything. So God gave them what they wanted. But there was a price. They each got an empty heart. They lost their passion for life. It always happens when we go our own way. A selfish person will always move outside God's plan and discover a wasteland. So please be careful of what you ask for. You may get it. Then you will have a bottomless heart to fill. And you don't want that.

What is the use of praying if at the very moment of prayer,
we have so little confidence in God that we are
busy planning our own kind of answer to our prayer?
— *Thomas Merton*

*B*arnabas wanted to take John along, the John nicknamed Mark. But Paul wouldn't have him; he wasn't about to take along a quitter who, as soon as the going got tough, had jumped ship on them in Pamphylia.

— *Acts 15:37-38*, MSG

NINETY-EIGHT
How to Fit In

It is true. John Mark quit. He jumped ship on the first missionary journey. He may have had a hard time fitting in. He may have been shy. He may have talked too much. Who knows? But his actions caused a split. It was clear that John Mark did not fit into Paul's second missionary plan.

You will have a hard time fitting in and finding good friends. Do not be alarmed if, like John Mark, you are disliked by a certain group. That's okay. Find at least one person who likes you. John Mark did. Barnabas believed in John Mark enough to part ways with Paul. He helped him fit in.

Never try to win the heart of a group. There will always be people you will clash with. So find one person you are compatible with and make friends. It will produce opportunities for other relationships.

> A friend is one who knows us, but loves us anyway.
> — *Fr. Jerome Cummings*

*W*hy, you do not even know what will
happen tomorrow. What is your life?
You are a mist that appears for
a little while and then vanishes.

— *James 4:14, NIV*

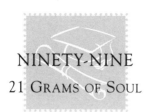

NINETY-NINE
21 Grams of Soul

It is the weight of a stack of five nickels—the sum of all our fears. It is the weight that everybody loses at the moment of death. It is the 21 grams of you that makes all the difference. It is what you should stake your life on. Every decision you make will either be against or for the eternal—21 grams. Money is nice. Fine jewelry is stunning. But the 21 grams is all that really matters. The weight of your soul will go somewhere. May it have an eternal rest with God.

So the question of utmost importance is: "How long will we get to carry it around in this life?" If you can answer this question, you do not need faith. But no one has the answer, except God. Our life is but a mist waiting to evaporate.

The one thing we yearn for in our living days, that makes us
sigh and groan and undergo sweet nauseas of all kinds,
is the remembrance of some lost bliss that was probably
experienced in the womb and can only be reproduced
(though we hate to admit) in death. But who wants to die?
—*Jack Kerouac, On the Road*

*S*oul, you've been rescued from death;
Eye, you've been rescued from tears;
And you, Foot, were kept from stumbling.

— Psalm 116:8, MSG

ONE-HUNDRED

It All Goes Back in the Box

*A*braham Lincoln once said, "Once the game is over, the king and the pawn go back in the same box." That's life. Everything we own, every award we have won, every fiber of our being will go back in the box one day. Some boxes will be pine or mahogany. Others will be exquisite metal with rich color. But a box is a box. And we will be the contents.

We have to think about this. If today were your day, how would you be remembered? What would be said about your life? I know it is hard to fathom. Yet it is truth. The king and the pawn will be placed in the same dirt. Everything will go back in the box. And there is only one thing that will not be there. It is our soul.

> Let us so live that when we come to die
> even the undertaker will be sorry.
> — *Mark Twain*

About the Author:

Robert Stofel is a native of Franklin, Tennessee. He has written for *St. Anthony's Messenger* and numerous university journals across the country. He won an award in the 2000 *Writer's Digest* Writing Competition for his story, "Post-it Notes to God at the Edge of Faulkner's Yard." He has spoken to thousands of students and has been the keynote speaker at Youth Encounter in Brisbane, Australia.